THE

APPLE-VISION PRO

VS.

META-QUEST 3

GUIDE

A Comprehensive Comparison
Guide on the Two Most
Advanced AR and VR
Technology

JOHNNY MAX CARSON

This BOOK belongs to

_____

_____

From:

_____

Signature/Date:

_____

TABLE OF CONTENTS

THE

APPLE VISION PRO

Apple Vision Pro marks a significant leap forward in the realm of mixed reality, blending digital content seamlessly with the real world. Announced in June 2023 and launched in February 2024, this cutting-edge headset represents Apple's first major venture into a new product category since the release of the Apple Watch in 2015. With its innovative features, advanced hardware, and user-centric design, the Vision Pro sets a new standard for immersive computing experiences.

Development

The journey towards the creation of the Apple Vision Pro began with strategic acquisitions and talent acquisitions. Apple's acquisition of Metaio, a German augmented reality (AR) company, in 2015 laid the foundation for its exploration into mixed reality technologies. This move was followed by the recruitment of key personnel, including Mike Rockwell and Jeff Norris, who played pivotal roles in driving the development of ARKit and the vision for the mixed-reality headset.

Despite facing challenges such as changes in leadership and technical hurdles, Apple's commitment to innovation remained unwavering. The departure of Jony Ive in 2019 and the subsequent leadership changes posed challenges, but the vision persisted under the stewardship of Evans Hankey and Geoff Stahl. The acquisition of Canadian MR company Vrvana in 2017 further enriched Apple's expertise in augmented and mixed reality technologies, paving the way for groundbreaking advancements in hardware and software integration.

Unveiling and Release

The anticipation surrounding the Apple Vision Pro reached a crescendo when it was unveiled at the 2023 Worldwide Developers Conference. With CEO Tim Cook leading the presentation, Apple showcased the device's capabilities, signaling its commitment to redefining the future of computing. The announcement sparked excitement among developers, content creators, and consumers alike, setting the stage for a transformative launch.

The release of the Vision Pro in the United States on February 2, 2024, marked a milestone in the evolution of mixed reality technologies. Pre-orders, which began on January 19, 2024, exceeded expectations, with initial shipments selling out within minutes. The overwhelming demand underscored the appetite for immersive computing experiences and validated Apple's strategic investment in mixed reality.

Key Features

At the heart of the Apple Vision Pro lies a host of groundbreaking features that redefine how users interact with digital content:

1. Spatial Computing: The Vision Pro transcends traditional notions of virtual and augmented reality, offering a spatial computing experience where digital media seamlessly integrates with the real world. Users can interact with virtual elements using motion gestures, eye tracking, and speech recognition, blurring the lines between the physical and digital realms.

2. VisionOS: Powered by visionOS, a mixed-reality operating system derived from iOS frameworks, the Vision Pro delivers a fluid and intuitive user experience. The 3D user interface facilitates multitasking through floating windows, providing users with unparalleled flexibility and control over their digital environment.

3. Optic ID: The device's iris scanner, known as Optic ID, utilizes LEDs and infrared cameras to authenticate users, akin to the Face ID feature on iPhones. This innovative technology ensures seamless and secure access to the device's features and content, enhancing user privacy and security.

4. EyeSight: EyeSight, a unique feature of the Vision Pro, displays a rendering of the user's avatar's eyes on the front of the headset. This not only enhances communication and social interaction but also serves as a visual indicator of the user's level of immersion in the mixed-reality environment.

5. Advanced Hardware: The Vision Pro boasts an array of advanced hardware components, including micro-OLED displays, sensors, microphones, and cameras. These components work in concert to deliver crisp visuals, immersive audio, and precise tracking, ensuring a seamless and immersive mixed-reality experience.

Specifications

The Apple Vision Pro's specifications underscore its commitment to performance, quality, and user experience:

- Curved laminated glass display

- Aluminum frame with a flexible cushion interior

- Five sensors, six microphones, and 12 cameras for tracking and interaction

- Two 1.41-inch micro-OLED displays with a total of 23 megapixels

- Apple M2 chip for seamless performance and efficiency

- Internal storage options ranging from 256 GB to 1 TB

- Removable, adjustable headband for a comfortable fit

- Eye tracking system utilizing LEDs and infrared cameras

- Optic ID iris scanner for secure authentication

- Speaker integrated into the headband for immersive audio

Accessories

The Apple Vision Pro offers a range of accessories designed to enhance the user experience:

- Travel bag: A stylish and functional accessory for storing and transporting the headset

- ZEISS optical inserts: Custom-designed inserts for users with farsightedness, ensuring optimal visual clarity and comfort

- Light seal and light seal cushion: Accessories designed to enhance comfort and immersion during extended use

- Battery holder: An essential accessory for extending the device's battery life, providing users with uninterrupted access to immersive experiences

Additionally, a developer-specific adapter is available for registered Apple Developer accounts, enabling enhanced connectivity and diagnostic capabilities for developers.

Software

VisionOS serves as the backbone of the Apple Vision Pro, offering a rich and immersive software experience:

- 3D user interface: Navigated via finger tracking, eye tracking, and speech recognition, the interface provides intuitive control and interaction with digital content.

- App compatibility: visionOS supports a wide range of apps from the App Store, as well as selected iOS and iPadOS apps, ensuring access to a diverse ecosystem of content and services.

- Screen mirroring: The operating system enables seamless screen mirroring to other Apple devices, extending the device's capabilities and enhancing productivity.

- Peripheral compatibility: visionOS supports external peripherals such as the Magic Keyboard, Magic Trackpad, and gamepads, enabling versatile input options for users.

- Developer tools: Developers have access to a robust set of tools and frameworks for creating immersive experiences, and fostering innovation and creativity in mixed-reality development.

The Apple Vision Pro represents a paradigm shift in the world of mixed reality, offering users an unparalleled blend of digital and physical experiences. With its innovative features, advanced hardware, and intuitive software, the Vision Pro redefines how we interact with technology, opening up new possibilities for creativity, productivity, and entertainment.

As Apple continues to push the boundaries of innovation, the Vision Pro stands as a testament to the company's commitment to shaping the future of computing.

THE

META QUEST 3

The Meta Quest 3, developed by Reality Labs, a division of Meta Platforms, represents a significant milestone in the evolution of virtual reality (VR) headsets. Unveiled on June 1, 2023, and released on October 10 of the same year, the Quest 3 builds upon the success of its predecessors, incorporating updated hardware, advanced sensors, and innovative software features to deliver an immersive and seamless VR experience. In this comprehensive overview, we delve into the hardware specifications, software integration, release details, and reception of the Meta Quest 3.

Hardware Specifications

The Meta Quest 3 features a sleek and refined design, combining elements from the Quest 2 and Quest Pro to deliver a premium VR headset experience. One of the most notable upgrades is the use of a pair of LCDs with a per-eye resolution of 2064×2208, surpassing the resolution of the Quest 2. This increase in resolution enhances visual clarity and fidelity, allowing users to immerse themselves in rich and detailed virtual environments.

The front face of the headset is adorned with three "pills," each containing essential sensors and cameras for tracking and mixed reality functionality. The outer pills house monochrome cameras for positional tracking, while the center pill contains a depth sensor, enabling enhanced spatial awareness. Additionally, the color cameras in the outer pills enable mixed reality pass-throughs, allowing users to seamlessly blend virtual content with their real-world environment.

Under the hood, the Quest 3 is powered by the Snapdragon XR2 Gen 2, a high-performance system-on-chip manufactured by Qualcomm. This chipset offers more than double the raw graphics performance of its predecessor, ensuring smooth and responsive VR experiences. The headset ships with the new "Touch Plus" controllers, featuring infrared sensors for precise tracking and a redesigned form factor for improved ergonomics.

Software Integration

The Meta Quest 3 is designed to be backward compatible with all Quest 2 software, ensuring a seamless transition for existing users. However, developers have the opportunity to optimize their software for the Quest 3, leveraging its higher-resolution displays and enhanced graphics capabilities. This optimization may include higher fidelity graphics, improved performance, and enhanced gameplay experiences tailored specifically for the Quest 3's hardware.

In addition to backward compatibility, Meta has announced plans for a lineup of new apps and games to coincide with the Quest 3's launch. Titles such as Assassin's Creed Nexus VR, Asgard's Wrath 2, and PowerWash Simulator promise to deliver immersive gaming experiences that showcase the capabilities of the Quest 3. Furthermore, the integration of Xbox Cloud Gaming as an app for the Quest 3 expands the device's entertainment options, allowing users to access a vast library of Xbox games in VR.

Release

The Meta Quest 3 generated significant anticipation ahead of its release, with early hands-on reports praising its upgraded hardware and improved mixed reality passthrough mode. The headset was made available for pre-order on September 28, 2023, with orders shipping the following month. The 128 GB and 512 GB models were priced at US$499.99 and US$649.99, respectively, with all pre-order units bundled with Asgard's Wrath 2.

Reception

Initial reviews of the Meta Quest 3 were largely positive, with reviewers praising its technical advancements and ergonomic improvements. Wired highlighted the upgraded hardware and comfortable fit of the Quest 3, while Polygon noted its completeness out of the box and potential for enhanced gaming experiences with optimized software.

However, some reviewers pointed out shortcomings in controller tracking accuracy and the limited use of mixed reality in available applications. Despite these criticisms, the Quest 3 received accolades for its overall performance and potential to drive further growth in the VR market.

Meta Quest 3 represents a significant leap forward in virtual reality technology, combining cutting-edge hardware with innovative software to deliver an immersive and compelling VR experience. With its high-resolution displays, advanced sensors, and extensive library of content, the Quest 3 has the potential to redefine how we interact with digital content and shape the future of virtual reality. As Meta continues to iterate and innovate, the Quest 3 stands as a testament to the company's commitment to pushing the boundaries of immersive technology.

A COMPREHENSIVE COMPARISON:

APPLE VISION PRO

VS.

META QUEST 3

In the rapidly evolving landscape of augmented reality (AR) and virtual reality (VR) technology, the Apple Vision Pro and the Meta Quest 3 stand out as two formidable contenders, each vying for dominance in the immersive computing space.

As consumers navigate the plethora of options available, a thorough understanding of the differences and similarities between these cutting-edge devices is essential.

From hardware specifications to software integration, design aesthetics to pricing, this comprehensive comparison explores every facet of the Apple Vision Pro and the Meta Quest 3, providing insights into their respective strengths and weaknesses.

Hardware:

At the heart of any AR or VR headset lies its hardware, dictating performance, visual quality, and overall user experience. The Meta Quest 3 and the Apple Vision Pro employ distinct hardware architectures, each tailored to optimize specific functionalities.

The Meta Quest 3 features a utilitarian design, characterized by a plain white plastic front adorned with three pill-shaped modules housing essential sensors and cameras. The headset boasts dual LCD pancake lenses, offering a per-eye resolution of 2064 x 2208 pixels for sharp visuals and a wide field of view. Powered by the Qualcomm Snapdragon XR2 Gen 2 chipset with 8GB of RAM, the Quest 3 delivers robust performance for gaming and multimedia experiences.

In contrast, the Apple Vision Pro exudes elegance with its sleek black glass-like front housing a myriad of sensors. The micro-OLED displays offer a per-eye resolution of approximately 4K, delivering unparalleled visual clarity and detail. Powered by Apple's proprietary M2 chip and R1 chip, the Vision Pro promises unrivaled performance and efficiency, optimized for seamless integration with entertainment and productivity applications.

Software Integration:

Beyond hardware, software integration plays a crucial role in shaping the user experience of AR and VR headsets. The Meta Quest 3 runs on Meta's Quest operating system, based on Android, providing a user-friendly interface and seamless access to a vast library of VR content. Despite occasional software limitations, the Quest OS offers a robust platform for gaming, multimedia, and mixed-reality experiences.

In contrast, the Apple Vision Pro leverages Apple's VisionOS, a proprietary operating system tailored for immersive computing. Drawing from Apple's extensive ecosystem of applications and services, VisionOS promises seamless integration with entertainment, productivity, and creativity tools. While details about VisionOS are scarce, Apple's track record of software optimization and ecosystem integration instills confidence in Vision Pro's software capabilities.

Design Aesthetics:

D esign aesthetics not only influence the visual appeal but also impact comfort and usability. The Meta Quest 3 adopts a utilitarian design ethos, featuring a white plastic front adorned with minimalist sensors and a Y-style head strap for stability. The IPD adjustment wheel and ergonomic controllers enhance user comfort and control during extended VR sessions.

Conversely, the Apple Vision Pro epitomizes sophistication with its sleek black enclosure and minimalist design elements. The single strap design, embedded speakers, and adjustable fit dial prioritize comfort and aesthetics, catering to discerning users seeking a premium AR experience.

Battery Life and Performance:

Battery life and performance are paramount considerations for immersive computing devices, affecting usability and convenience. The Meta Quest 3 offers an estimated battery life of 2.4 hours during gaming sessions, powered by a robust chipset optimized for efficiency. The Snapdragon XR2 Gen 2 chipset delivers smooth performance and video pass-through with minimal latency, enhancing the overall VR experience.

In comparison, the Apple Vision Pro's battery life remains undisclosed, but reports suggest a similar runtime to the Meta Quest 3. However, the Vision Pro's performance benefits from Apple's M2 chip and R1 chip, promising superior processing power and energy efficiency. While benchmarks and real-world performance tests are pending, Apple's reputation for hardware optimization instills confidence in the Vision Pro's performance capabilities.

Display and Audio Quality:

Visual clarity and audio immersion are essential aspects of the AR and VR experience, shaping immersion and realism. The Meta Quest 3's dual LCD pancake lenses offer sharp visuals with a wide field of view, complemented by near-field speakers for spatial audio. While the Quest 3's 120Hz refresh rate enhances motion smoothness, its LCDs may fall short of the color accuracy and contrast offered by OLED technology.

In contrast, the Apple Vision Pro's micro-OLED displays boast superior color accuracy and contrast, delivering stunning visuals with lifelike detail. The embedded speakers provide spatial audio support, enhancing immersion and realism for entertainment and productivity applications. While specific details about FOV and audio fidelity are pending, Apple's emphasis on quality suggests a premium audiovisual experience with the Vision Pro.

Camera Technology and Mixed Reality:

Pass-through cameras and mixed reality capabilities redefine the boundaries between the virtual and real worlds, enabling immersive experiences and real-world interactions. The Meta Quest 3 features front-facing cameras with a depth sensor, facilitating mixed reality experiences with natural color reproduction and spatial awareness. Meta's commitment to mixed reality is evident through a range of MR experiences tailored for the Quest 3.

Conversely, the Apple Vision Pro boasts a total of 12 cameras, including LIDAR cameras and motion sensors, enabling precise tracking and 3D information capture. While specific details about mixed reality experiences are limited, Apple's focus on spatial video and entertainment suggests a robust framework for immersive content creation and consumption.

Price and Accessibility:

Perhaps the most significant differentiator between the Meta Quest 3 and the Apple Vision Pro lies in their price and accessibility. The Meta Quest 3 is widely available, with a price point of $500, making it a more affordable option for consumers seeking a high-quality VR experience. In contrast, the Apple Vision Pro commands a premium price tag of $3,499, positioning it as a luxury product targeted toward discerning users willing to invest in cutting-edge technology.

CONCLUSION

The Apple Vision Pro and the Meta Quest 3 represent two distinct approaches to immersive computing, each with its unique strengths and weaknesses. While the Meta Quest 3 excels in affordability, gaming, and mixed reality experiences, the Apple Vision Pro sets a new standard for visual fidelity, design elegance, and ecosystem integration. Ultimately, the choice between these two devices depends on factors such as budget, use case, and brand preference. Whether you prioritize gaming immersion or entertainment sophistication, both the Apple Vision Pro and the Meta Quest 3 push the boundaries of what's possible in immersive computing, heralding a new era of AR and VR technology.

NOTES

NOTES

NOTES

NOTES

NOTES

www.ingramcontent.com/pod-product-compliance
Lightning Source LLC
LaVergne TN
LVHW051634050326
832903LV00033B/4750